Jack Versus
The Peanut

Jack Versus The Peanut

Life In A Peanut Study

Jack Cole

ISBN: 0692954651
ISBN 13: 9780692954652
Library of Congress Control Number: 2017914855
Jack Cole, Boca Raton, FL

June, 2016

My name is Jack Cole. I am almost ten and live in Florida. I'm really busy with school, golf, tennis, books, iPad, and Tae Kwon Do. There's something else you should know about me - I am really allergic to peanuts and will be part of a study to help people with my allergy. There are a lot of us around – like over 3,000,000 people in America are allergic to peanuts, nuts, or both. Because of that, I thought it was a good idea to write about my experience with this allergy and with this study, so people can learn what it's like. I'll take you on an adventure – my adventure – into the great, wide world of children's allergy studies. I

Jack Cole

hope you enjoy it, and I hope the study helps my peanut allergy and everyone else's.

This is me:

1. So, what exactly is a Peanut?

Did you know that a peanut isn't a real nut? It's actually something called a legume. It's related to peas, not to cashews or almonds. I'm only allergic to peanuts, but many people have both peanut and nut allergies together because the proteins are similar.   I actually have to eat tree nuts like almonds and pistachios, so I don't develop an allergy to them.

2. What Does It Mean That I'm Allergic To Peanuts?

An allergic reaction happens when things that people are allergic to get into their bodies. This usually happens by eating them, but sometimes people have a reaction just by breathing in the thing they're allergic to. Your body thinks you've eaten something dangerous, so it starts producing something called *histamines* to protect itself. Histamines are chemicals that your body makes and puts into your bloodstream, but those chemicals can make your body go haywire — your eyes, nose, lungs, skin, and stomach. People who have food allergies can have different reactions at different times, but the worst immediate reaction you can have is *anaphylaxis* — a big word for something really bad — I mean life or death. It's when all those histamines come and just flood your body, which can stop you from breathing, make you vomit, and drop your pulse. The reaction can start with very small symptoms that get worse and worse. If you don't get help right away and get to the hospital, you can die. The scariest thing is you don't know when you'll have just the small symptoms by themselves or when they will turn into something like anaphylaxis! When you are allergic to peanuts, even a small amount of peanut can cause a huge reaction. If you want more information on this, see KidsHealth. Org. It's great at explaining all the science and medical stuff.

Unlike some other allergies, a peanut allergy is usually with you for life. It's really annoying and scary to think that I will have this allergy with me forever (unless I'm one of the lucky ones). That's why I am participating in a clinical study of the "peanut patch." If this is successful, it could make me less sensitive if I accidentally eat peanuts. The hope is that after some time, I'll be able to eat up to 5 peanuts without reacting! I can't even imagine what that would be like – to not worry about eating a speck of peanut and if that would mean I could die.

3. How'd I Know I Was Allergic?

The first time I had peanuts for sure was when my mom gave them to me when I was three. I don't remember it so well, but I know she gave me some almonds one week, then walnuts a second week, then peanuts on the third week. A few minutes later, I remember I vomited all over the kitchen floor and my mom ran upstairs to get a medicine called Benadryl. She gave me the medicine, threw us in the car, and raced to the doctor. That's when I was diagnosed. My mom told me that this was a problem a lot of kids have now, and we just had to watch out for eating peanuts.

4. Run-Ins With and Running Away From My Enemy - The Peanut

The best way to avoid a peanut reaction is to avoid foods when you don't know the ingredients. Things like candy, ice cream, and baked goods that all look delicious can be really dangerous. We have to check labels on everything and only eat at restaurants where we know they are really good about food allergies. I'm very aware of reading labels on anything I eat. If it doesn't have a label, and I'm not sure, I don't eat it. I'm so used to looking at ingredients that if I could somehow cure my peanut allergy, I would still read the labels. I can't help it!

Even though my family is super-careful about avoiding them, I have accidentally eaten peanuts. When that happens, my mouth and tongue can feel weird and/or tingly, my stomach can hurt or bother me, or I can get big red itchy hives on my face. Sometimes I don't even know the hives are there - until they get itchy! If this happens, I have to take the Benadryl to clear up histamines in my body. Benadryl's either a tablet I chew up or a liquid. Both taste like grape or bubblegum. It's pretty good. I can taste that grape flavor for a long time in my mouth. The medicine makes most people tired, but I have never let myself fall asleep from taking Benadryl. I don't want to miss out on any fun things because of a medicine.

I'm lucky because up until now my reaction has never been really bad, but it could be. This makes me really nervous. I try not to think about it all the time, but like I said before, peanuts could make me stop breathing. If that ever happened, we would need to use something called an Epi-Pen or an Auvi-Q, which has a medicine called epinephrine in it. They are shots with a small needle that I would inject into my thigh, and they would help me start breathing well again. I can do it right through my clothing. After that, I would rush to the hospital or get an ambulance, so the doctors could drip the medicine right into my arm through an even smaller needle.

My allergy can make things like going on an airplane terrifying. We only fly airlines like JetBlue and Delta, which are really considerate and let us go on the plane early, so my parents can wipe down our seats. When we get on the plane, we tell the flight attendants about my allergy again, and they don't serve peanuts during the flight and ask people around me not to eat peanuts during the flights. Once we complete these steps, I smile because I know I'm safe. Thanks Delta and JetBlue! My mom used to give me Benadryl before every flight until my allergist said it was a bad idea because it's better to know if I'm having a reaction and then give the Benadryl.

We take all these precautions, but things can still happen. On a very nice, sunny day, my family drove to the airport to head home after our vacation. My dad and sister Morgan dropped my mom and I off at the departure terminal with the luggage and went to return the rental car. We got our tickets from a computer and breezed through security.

On this day, my dad and Morgan met up with us at the gate, and my dad handed me a bag that smelled great.

"Here, try a bagel. I talked to the manager at the store. No peanuts," Dad said.

I took a few bites, and it did taste great. I was so hungry. A few minutes later, I saw my mom look at me in a really worried kind of way.

"You have hives on your face," she said, quickly searching for Benadryl in her bag as she said it. She ripped open the package and handed me 2 tablets. I chewed them just as the person at the gate announced that our plane was beginning to pre-board passengers.

Usually, I rush to pre-board. That day, though, I started crying because I didn't even want to get on the plane. What if I had a bad reaction, and we were thousands of feet in the sky? How could they get me to a hospital?

"I'll stay with Jack here for the night, and you two go home," my dad said, starting to separate my stuff from my sister's as the boarding area got really crowded.

"The hives are going away, but, okay, we'll pick you up tomorrow at the airport," my mom said, handing my dad the Epi-Pens in case he needed them.

I was feeling better and calming down. I could feel the Benadryl making me a little sleepy already. "Wait," I said, fighting the last of my tears.

"I can go." I started walking to the boarding area. I knew my parents wouldn't let me go if they thought I was in danger. My mom basically stared at my face the entire flight to make sure I was okay. When I got home, she gave me more Benadryl to make sure I didn't have a second reaction. I lived happily ever after. :)

You can see - I have to be careful all the time. At baseball games, I'm really nervous but try not to be. I see peanuts and shells everywhere. We try to sit near people who aren't eating peanuts or else the baseball game gets nerve-wracking for me — and not because of the actual game.

School is another place where I have to watch out because lots of kids like peanut butter and might not think about the fact that I can react to their food. At the beginning of third grade, my teachers made a sign saying that our classroom was nut free. They also sent a notice to all the parents of the kids, asking them not to bring nut products to class for snacks or parties. My teachers always helped me make sure I was safe eating at snack time and in the cafeteria.

During the year, I need to make sure that other people's snacks don't contain traces of peanuts. If their snack says *may contain peanuts*, I just ask them to wash their hands after they eat. It's easy because the kids in my class are really good sports about not eating nut products until after school. Sometimes when I didn't look, a friend would come up to me and say something like,

"Look, I think my granola might have peanuts," and then he'd eat it away from me and wash his hands after. Most of the time that happens, though, it was just "may contain peanuts". They are really good friends.

At lunch, I have to make sure things I eat don't have peanuts. This is easy because I know the head of the kitchen. He's always helpful and tells me there are no peanuts in the food I want to eat, but I double check with him just in case. He never minds me asking and always says,

"If there are nuts, there's a sign saying that the food contains nuts."

Usually, I'll read the sign and see that it contains walnuts or pistachios or something. I still stay away from those foods, though, because those nuts could have been made in a place where they mix nuts with peanuts.

The biggest bummer, though, is when people bring in special treats for their birthdays. About 2/3 of the time, I can't eat whatever they bring in, even though it looks delicious. My mom always makes sure I have safe treats to eat instead, but a lot of times I feel excluded. Why do I have to eat cookies when everyone else is eating cupcakes? Even if Famous Amos cookies are delicious. My class always tries to include me. For example, a classmate will say something like,

"You can eat my cupcakes 'cause I double checked, and there are no nuts."

Even though I want to eat it, I see there are no labels to read. I'll say,

"I'm so sorry. It's just that I want to be extra, extra safe."

They always understand because they know how severe my allergy is. Just like everywhere else, except for home, I have to be so careful when I'm at school.

I'm happy people try to make me feel better about my allergy. It's something that's always in the back of my head. When I was little, I always thought about my throat feeling weird at restaurants. This was a bad habit because I always worried and wound up having false alarms – like thinking my tongue felt weird or felt hives on my face that didn't exist. It's really annoying. Sort of like the allergy affects my mind and not just my body. Most of the time I force myself not to think about my allergy when I'm eating, even though one time I did have a reaction from eating at my favorite restaurants, and we never went back again.

5. The Study

Because my allergy has a way of sneaking itself into pretty much everything I do, my parents have been looking for a way to help me for years. They learned about something called "oral immunotherapy" a while ago. This means you build up the amount of peanut you can eat slowly over time, so your body gets used to it. My parents thought this was a great idea, but really risky. What if I took a dose and had an anaphylactic reaction? What if I had a reaction in my sleep? It didn't seem worth that big a risk. I also didn't like the idea of eating peanuts all the time. We all agreed it wasn't a good solution for me.

Then, my mom started reading about an idea that sounded less scary to us. They were doing a study where they put a patch on kids' backs, so they would become less sensitive to peanuts. The risk of anaphylaxis was much lower. This sounded amazing, but the problem was getting into a study. We live in Florida, and no hospitals in Florida or even Georgia participated in the study. My mom started looking around the country. Mt. Sinai in New York had hundreds of kids on a waiting list to get into their peanut patch study. John Hopkins in Maryland was full also, and so was the Children's Hospital in Philadelphia. UNC was all filled. Pittsburgh had too many kids, too. It seemed impossible. There are so many children who need help with their peanut allergy. We were beginning to give up hope when my mom e-mailed a hospital in Boston that had just started to participate in the study, and the doctor e-mailed her right back. I was in the middle of Tae Kwon Do when she whispered to me,

"We may get Boston. We'll get you up there for some tests."

My heart felt fluttery. I knew exactly what she meant — there were openings for a study in Boston. I was so excited that I might get the chance to lessen my allergy. When we found out I could go for a screening to see if the study would accept me, I couldn't believe it. Even though this wouldn't cure my allergy, it could help, so if I eat something with peanuts accidentally, the reaction wouldn't kill me. That would mean that maybe I could eat things that "May contain peanuts" or made "in a facility that processes peanuts". It would mean I could go back to my favorite restaurant. It would mean I would feel a whole lot safer.

6. Traveling to Boston

As my dad and I boarded the A320 to Boston two weeks later, my head was spinning with questions,

"Would the doctors and nurses be nice? What would the hospital be like?"

My dad wiped down our seats, and we were off for a two-day trip. When we landed, we took a train into Boston. I was amazed by the city. I saw huge buildings and so many buses on the street. It was June, and the weather was awe-some. My dad made the trip so much fun. We got to visit the Boston Aquarium and saw an Imax movie about the Galapagos Islands. After, we went to eat dinner at Legal Seafood. They were very careful about my allergy, so I felt safe. The next morning we took the train to the Science Center before my first visit for the study. We were so busy, I barely had time to think about my appointment, which was just a couple hours away.

My dad and I walked into one of the hospital entrances, which looked like a clump of connected buildings that went on forever. It looked tall, kind of old, and really busy. My heart pounded. I was going to my peanut study screening! I was really here! I got off the elevator on the 13th floor, and my dad checked me in at the reception desk. A few minutes later, I walked into a check-up room, which looked like a room in any doctor's office except there were more com-puters. Guess this is where we do everything, I thought to myself. I met a lot of people who helped in the study: nurs-es, people in charge of organizing the study, and the doctor. The doctor introduced himself to me and my dad and told us about the study and the risks of what could happen dur-ing the screening. He said there were some things he talked to all his patients about. First, he said the screening was to make sure that I was allergic to peanuts. Well that's not a problem, I thought to myself. Then he said he needed to make sure I was healthy. I had just had my annual checkup with my doctor, so I felt pretty good about that too. Next, he told me about the food challenge that took place over two separate days. On one day, they would give me food with no peanuts, but the other day the food would have some peanut mixture in it. He said that the worst possible thing that could happen is I would need to take an Epinephrine shot, which would help me if I couldn't breathe. Wait a minute! I thought. That doesn't sound so good. But I didn't say anything.

Finally, he talked about the patch. If I got into the study, there was a 2/3 chance that I'd get the real drug. Even if I didn't get the real patch at first, I would definitely get the real thing after the first year of the study. I felt nervous to get the actual peanut patch, even if I had to go through that really bad-sounding food challenge. He said we would come to Boston for at least 12 visits to check on my patch and for check-ups and a second food challenge. He also said that if my skin got irritated, it would most likely mean that I got the real thing. I felt like this was almost too much information at once, but I just wanted to keep going for a chance at that patch.

Another nice nurse came in and took my blood. I barely felt it because she was amazing at drawing blood. Next, the nurse said,

"We are going to give you a skin test. Do you know what that is?"

"I forgot," I admitted.

She explained: We will give you 3 skin pricks with liquids on them. One has peanut, one with saltwater, and one with histamine. We'll see how you react."

This was my reaction. The one on top was the peanut:

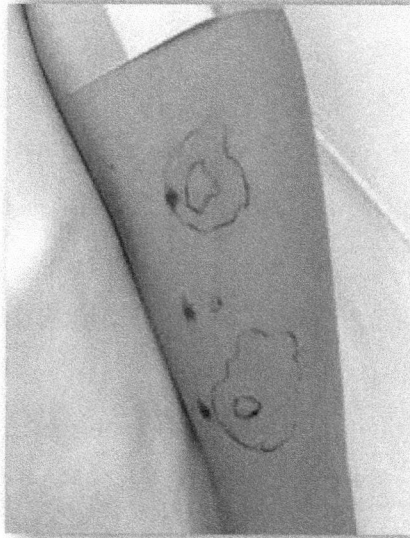

Unlike the blood test, the pricks really hurt! For 3 seconds it was horrible. Then it got better. After the nurse stuck the little needles into my arm, the histamine and the

peanut itched like crazy! They waited 15 minutes and then circled the reactions with a pen. It felt like forever until they wiped off the itchy liquid. It was pretty clear that my skin didn't like peanuts. They started to ask questions about my peanut allergy. I tried to answer all the questions with accuracy. Then they gave me three sheets of paper to answer. These were fun. For some questions, they made Dad leave to make sure that no one was forcing me to do the study. Believe me – I wanted to do it! Then they gave me a whacky breathing test that took me a while to figure out. It was called a spirometry test, and I blew into this tube attached to a video screen. If I blew it hard enough, a wolf blew a pig's hut over. Once I figured out how to blow into the tube correctly, they said I passed. The nurses said I was really healthy, and I could move on to the next part of the screening: the food challenge. Yikes!

"Yay," I said, trying to sound excited, but really nervous. I thought it was a good idea not to think about the food challenge at all until we came back to Boston.

My dad and I went back to Boston the next week for the food challenge. I kept wondering – was I going to get the placebo – that has no peanut - or the peanut the first day? I was about to find out! I was nervous because I didn't know what would happen when I got the peanut. I spent my whole life avoiding peanuts, and now I have to eat them! We rode up the elevator to the 13th floor and checked in. A minute later, the nurse said to come into the room where they would start the challenge. They quickly did a small check up and handed me the first dose. I looked down at the red Jell-O on the spoon.

"Should I eat it?" I asked, sort of hoping my dad would say I shouldn't.

"Yes," my dad said.

I put the spoon in my mouth. It tasted like liquid cherry pudding. It wasn't that bad. My dad was watching me the entire time. After a few minutes, he said,

"No hives. You feel ok?"

"Totally fine."

But I knew that the reaction could be later. A nurse stayed in my room the entire time and checked my temperature, pulse and blood pressure every twenty minutes. Thirty minutes later, the nurse gave me a second dose, which would have more peanut in it. I felt a little more confident because I hadn't had a hive yet. I ate it. A little later, my dad said I still didn't have hives. We started watching The Lord of The Rings. This was actually kind of fun. Now, I was wondering if I got the placebo. That meant I would get the peanut at the next food challenge. Going into the third dose without a reaction made me feel more comfortable about not getting the peanut pudding. I ate the next dose without a reaction. Now, I really felt like I was safe for the day. I ate the last few doses and felt the same as I always do. My dad and I finished the movie because the doctors had to make sure I didn't have a delayed reaction. I was cleared after that — placebo city! I felt relief but also sort of dread.

Two days later, I was back on the elevator to the thirteenth floor. I took a deep breath, checked in, and headed to the same room. They did another physical exam to see how I was doing before I got the pudding. I was okay but felt really nervous and wanted to get the day over with. I think I had been thinking about it too much. The nurse handed me the first dose. I looked at my dad and swallowed it immediately. Might as well get it over with. I felt perfect, which was really weird. No reaction after a second or third dose. After twenty minutes, my dad said,

"I thought you were going to have an immediate reaction."

"Me too!" I said. The nurse laughed but couldn't say anything. No reaction, still? Could they have made a big mistake?

"Maybe they forgot to add the peanuts on both days!" I exclaimed. My dad shook his head and said,

"This is a good thing. You can tolerate more peanut than we thought!"

I took the fourth dose. Still no reaction, but by now the cherry pudding was tasting pretty disgusting. The fifth dose did not go as smoothly. A minute after I ate it, I got a really huge stomach-ache. I grimaced. The nurse took my pulse and said it went up a lot and that my face was red. The doctor came in and looked at my chart and then at me. My stomach hurt so much I was squirming in my chair.

"Please stop the test. Please stop the test," I thought to myself over and over.

The doctor agreed with my thoughts. He said something like, "He's having a big enough reaction. Benadryl now and no sixth dose. This is a positive response. You're welcome into the study."

My dad high-fived me. I felt so happy and relieved, but the Benadryl was a disgusting tasting bubble gum. I'm not a picky eater, but this was the worst taste ever. I wanted to spit it out, but I knew it would help my reaction to the peanut. Next time I'd ask my mom to give me the Benadryl she buys to bring along! The last three hours went by in a snap. I was okay! It was a little fun and a lot scary, but I was so happy to have that day done. The best part: I was in the study!

7. The Patch

On our last day in Boston, we went over to the hospital to get the patch applied to my back. My thoughts kept going a mile a minute. Was it going to hurt? Would I get the real medicine or a fake patch for a year? 13th floor here I come. I checked in and went to my room. It felt very familiar to me now.

The nurse came and smiled. She showed us to my room.

"How are you feeling today, Jack?"

"Great" I said.

"Fabulous," she said. "Could you lie on your stomach. I'll lift your shirt and place the patch on your back. Let's have your dad watch, so he knows how to do it." She showed me the patch, which looked like a see-through donut Band-Aid about an inch wide. I felt the nurse placing it on my back, and it didn't feel like anything.

"Every day, you'll switch the patch into six different spots on his back." The nurse said. "At first, it's for just six hours a day, and then it will go up to the entire day."

We stayed in the hospital for three hours after that. Studies have a lot of waiting time!

My dad looked at my back.

"It looks red under the patch," my dad said. "This could be the real deal."

This is what it looked like:

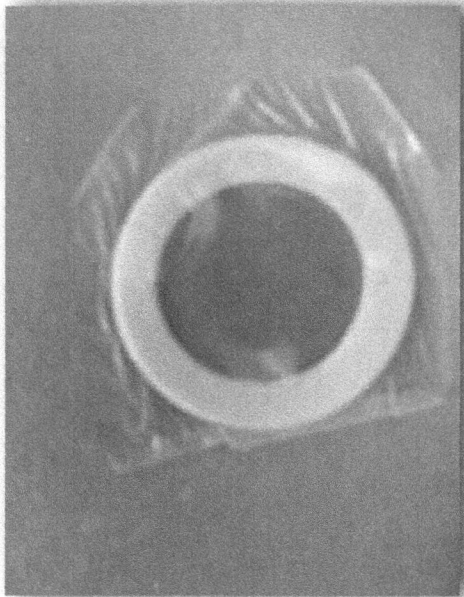

The nurse looked too and said something like: "Well, none of us know who gets the real drug and who gets the placebo. Still, it looks red, so that's something."

After my dad and I left, we went to a 7-11 to buy a few things. My back really started itching.

"It's really red now," my dad said.

8. Itchy Like Crazy

"Yes!" I said. This was great news. I am probably getting the drug. At least, I hoped this was true! That night my back was itchy, itchy, itchy. This was driving me crazy, but Dad said it was worth being itchy for helping my allergy. He rubbed my back to help with the itchiness. This would hopefully help me to eat five or six peanuts, I told myself. It was worth it.

After they put the patch on, I thought everything would be fine, maybe just a little rash or something where they put it on. Boy, was I wrong. After a few hours of the patch, my back wouldn't stop itching. At that instant, I knew that for at least a couple weeks, that was how my back was going to feel. It was hard not to be frustrated. Luckily, the doctor gave me hydrocortisone cream. When I got home and my mom applied it, I sighed with relief. I knew it would still itch, but not as much with the cream. I kept complaining about the itchiness for the next few days. I couldn't help it. I really hoped in a few weeks it felt better. Even as I'm writing this, my back is still red and itching. I really hope this goes away soon.

Six days after I put the patch on, my mom and I flew back up to Boston. Mom woke me up at 4:30 in the morning to catch a flight. We parked at the Fort Lauderdale airport and headed to security and then our gate. As always, JetBlue let us get on early to wipe down our seats. The 2 hours, 51 minutes to Boston (I timed it) went by quickly because I played on my iPad the whole time. Since I learned my way around

Boston the week before with my dad, I led my mom on the Transit (T) from the airport to The Cheesecake Factory. My mom looked a little confused after our third transfer on the T.

"Are you sure you know which way to go?" she asked.

"Trust me," I said.

We arrived at The Cheesecake Factory, and my mom was shocked at how much Romano-crusted chicken I ate.

"You must be really full," she said. "Let's walk to the hospital from here."

We walked past the Science Center and over the Charles River. Lots of people were running around the river. It was such a beautiful day. I showed her The Liberty Hotel where Dad and I had stayed. It used to be an old prison, and they still had bars on a lot of the windows.

"Pretty cool," my mom said, impressed.

9. Thirteenth Floor - Again

I led my mom through the hospital to the Allergy Floor. We checked in and after a few minutes, a nurse led me to a room with an armchair in it. There was another boy in another part of the room. It looked like he was doing a food challenge. There was a curtain between us, so it was hard to see. I sat down in the armchair, and the nurse took my pulse and temperature. Then I got up to get my height and weight.

"He probably hasn't grown much in the past six days," my mom joked.

"You never know!" I said.

The nurse said I looked good and looked at my back. She said the reaction looked about average. This was good news, but I couldn't believe how many itchy kids there must be walking around with patches on their backs. She recommended two medications to help with the itchiness and handed my mom a sheet of paper.

Next, the research coordinator came in to meet my mom and look at my back. She performed my favorite exam – the spirometry test – I really liked to see if I could knock down the hut where the pig is hiding. I blew the hut down twice, so my lungs were in good shape. This was a quick appointment – it lasted about an hour.

My mom and I bought the Zyrtec that the nurse had recommended, and we went back to the T for our trip back to the airport. While we sat on the plane, waiting for the rest of the passengers to board, the front of my shoulder started itching.

"Hey Mom, my shoulders itching," I said, showing her bumps that had come up on the front of my shoulder, near my chest.

My mom took a quick picture on her phone and immediately sent it to the doctor. She decided to give me Benadryl, since we were about to fly. It was the good tasting grape flavor! While the flight attendant made his safety announcements, the doctor called my mom.

"I already gave Jack some Benadryl, just in case," my mom said. The doctor said it was fine for me to fly. As I watched us take off into the sky, I really hoped my back would get less itchy soon.

My back at its worst:

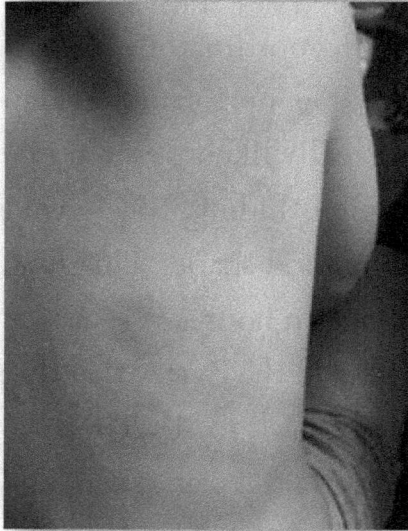

The next morning, my mom said to me,

"If this ever gets too uncomfortable for you, we're going to stop the study."

"I'll let you know, but it's not so bad," I said. "Let's see what happens in the next few weeks." I was trying to stay hopeful. It would be worth it in the end! I just had to keep reminding myself of that.

June, 2017

I. The End of Year One

Wow, a year zoomed by so quickly, and now it's already the beginning of June and I'm 10 ... just two more weeks until the next food challenge. Throughout the last year, I tolerated the patch (sometimes barely) and stayed in the study. I also went up to Boston three more times, so the doctors could take a peek at my patch and make sure everything looked okay. Those appointments were just like the ones I had described to you earlier: Questions, occasional skin test, some blood tests, and always checking my breathing level. Luckily, during the year my patch level has gone from a 3 out of 3 in itchiness, to a 0.5 in itchiness, but my back still gets pretty red wherever the patch goes.

Two weeks later I board the plane to go to the food challenge. I was beyond excited and wondering the same familiar questions. Will I be able to tolerate a lot of peanuts? Has my tolerance increased? We would soon find out. Our flight was completely uneventful. It was a 2hr and 38 minute flight (timed it again). After we landed in Boston, we took the blue line subway to our hotel. Our hotel was called The Bostonian, and it was in a great location in Boston. It was near Faneuil Hall, one of the most famous places in Boston. My dad and I decided to go and explore. The concierge recommended a place called Sail Loft. They had great seafood, and they took my allergy very seriously. I ate clam chowder with oyster crackers, shrimp, and sea scallops. My favorite was the clam chowder. My dad and I love to watch movies, so before we went to bed, we watched a movie called Mission Impossible 5.

2. Food Challenge Number Two

I slowly raised my head and realized it was already the next morning. I had slept well. The beds in the hotel were very comfortable. I quietly moved in my bed and waited a couple of minutes for my dad to wake up. When he did, I said, "Let's get a move on." I really wanted to get the real peanut on this day just to get it over with. My dad and I had some breakfast and then took the subway to the hospital. We went up to the 12th floor this time because they were renovating the 13th floor. The doctors took me into room

18, and my nurse performed all the normal procedures like taking height, weight, and blood pressure. Then, I took a blood test and a skin prick test. The nurse did a very good job of reducing the pain. Then she said," Here is dose one." Right then I realized the food challenge had just begun.

This food challenge was a little different. Instead of taking 6 doses, I had to take 8 doses, so the doctors could see my maximum tolerance to help with their research. I took the first dose. Gross, I thought. That yucky cherry liquid is still around! For now I wasn't worried because in the last food challenge I didn't react until the fifth dose. The first four doses went by quickly. Two hours later the nurse was saying, " Here's the fifth dose." I told her that this was where I had my reaction last time, so we should observe everything very carefully. Thirty minutes later, no reaction. So far so good. The sixth dose was even bigger! Still no reaction. It was exactly the same for the seventh and eighth doses. I was wondering, is this the placebo, or I am not that allergic anymore? We would have to find out on Wednesday.

3. The Day In-Between

It was Tuesday. That meant that today was a fun day! There were two things on our agenda for today. I wanted to go on a whale watch and go to Providence, so I could see my dad's old school, Brown. We went to Boston Harbor and bought tickets for a 10:00 whale watch. An hour into our trip, people spotted something in the water. It wasn't a whale. It was a shark! This shark was a basking shark, the second longest shark in the world. The trip continued, and we saw more whales and sharks. This had been a fun trip, but it was 1:30, and we needed to catch a 2:30 train. We bolted to the train station and made it just in time. An hour later, we were in Providence, RI. My dad showed me where he had his classes, the libraries, his dorm, and much more. I saw his old dorm room, but it was a huge mess! I loved seeing what his college was like. My dad and I caught the 5:20 train back to Boston, and we had Cheesecake Factory for dinner. Great day!

4. Food Challenge - The Real Deal

The next day was Wednesday. We needed to get an early move on today because our appointment was at 7:00 a.m. Let's do this! When we got to the hospital around 6:50, I was nervous and excited with all those question marks in my head. I went upstairs and took dose one at around 7:30. The nurse took my vital signs every twenty minutes. I had no reaction after four doses. The fifth dose was right in front of my face, and now it was time for me to take it. The cherry pudding tasted disgusting by now. Thirty minutes later and I didn't have a reaction. I took the sixth dose. My stomach started to hurt just a little bit. It got worse and worse. I went to the bathroom and that helped my stomach feel better. Then it hurt a little bit more. A nurse came in, and we talked about my options. She said I could stop, and stop the entire study, or continue. She said my reaction was not severe enough to stop the doses. My stomach feeling better again, I didn't want to drop out of the study, so I took dose 7 and no reaction! This is a miracle, I thought. Finally, I took dose 8. The last of all the doses! Seconds began to feel like minutes. I was getting worried. Half an hour later, no reaction. "HALLELUJAH," I yelled. Everyone laughed. I was so excited, but we were still watching just to be safe. An hour later, the doctor came in. He was telling my dad and me about the next food challenge. A second later, Boom. I threw up. My stomach hurt. I was having trouble breathing. The doctor yelled," Get the Epi-pen." They gave me the shot, a nebulizer, which helps you breathe better, and a lot of other medicines. I was cold and my nose was super stuffy. An hour later, I felt fine. The nurses explained to me that I had had an anaphylactic reaction. At least now I knew what it felt like to have one. It wasn't as scary as I thought it would be, but that's probably because I was surrounded by doctors and nurses. All the medicine made me really tired:

The doctor checked on me again and told me some exciting news. At the beginning of the study, I was only able to tolerate 1/3 of a peanut. Now I could tolerate 13 peanuts, and I reacted from 20 peanuts. I couldn't stop smiling. This was great! This entire study was worth it!! My dad and I watched The X-MEN, while we waited for the hospital to let me leave. I loved that movie. My dad brought me Blaze Pizza. This had been an exciting day. A really momentous day.

5. Here Comes Part Two

After I felt better, the doctor talked to us about continuing with Part 2 of the study. My dad signed the waiver, so I could keep going. For the next two years I'll receive the real peanut patch. It was funny because this whole year we knew I had gotten the real patch because my tolerance increased, but no one will say it for sure until November when the number that they assigned to me is "unblinded". That's when it will be official. But just for the record, I told you so beforehand!

It was time to go back home, but we stayed in Boston one more night just in case I had a second reaction to the food challenge. I didn't, and the next day the plane was at 8:30 a.m. The captain let me speak through the intercom while everyone else was boarding. Other than that, it was an uneventful flight. When we got home, my mom was so happy to see us. She had missed us just as much as we had missed her. No matter how great a trip I have had, I love coming back home from vacation and getting into my nice comfy bed. This had been a great first year. Now, the second year starts.

Uhh! I jerked awake. It was the middle of the night. 1:00 to be exact. I had a piercing headache. I tried to drink some water, but my head still felt really bad. I fell back asleep. I woke up with that headache still with me. Now, I felt nauseated. I went to go wake my mom and dad up, then ran to the bathroom to throw up. My mom gave me Benadryl, and I threw that up too! My mom brought me to the couch when I said I didn't have to throw up anymore. My dad covered me in a blanket, and my mom called the doctor. He told my mom that this reaction had nothing to do with my peanut exposure. It was probably dehydration or all that bad cherry pudding! I was relieved and felt better in a few hours. My mom made me drink tons of liquid that day. At the end of the day, I felt perfect, so I had a play date with my friend. I also had a tennis tournament the next day, so thank goodness I was okay for that.

That's it! This has been year one of my peanut study. This is how I battled the peanut and won (just a little bit). I hope you'll find a strategy to tackle your own allergy, and I hope my experience gives you an idea of what it's like to be in a study. Remember, not every experience is the same, so not everything that happened to me might happen to you. Whatever you are facing, I hope this can show you that it's okay to be nervous — new experiences can be scary but well worth the risk!